AT HOME

A VISIT IN FOUR LANGUAGES

by Esther Hautzig

illustrated by Aliki

THE MACMILLAN COMPANY · NEW YORK

COLLIER-MACMILLAN LIMITED · LONDON

The Macmillan Company, New York
Collier-Macmillan Canada, Ltd., Toronto, Ontario
Library of Congress catalog card number: 68-23063
Printed in the United States of America
FIRST PRINTING

French, Spanish and Russian words and phonetics by the editorial staff of Berlitz Publications, Inc.

For Dorothy and Ben
who made me
at home

Home is the best place in all the world.

It is wonderful to be together with your family in familiar comfortable rooms . . .

in Chicago

lamp
lampe
lahmp
lámpara
lahm-pah-rah
лампа
lahm-pah

clock
pendule
pahn-dewl
reloj
reh-lohkh
часы
chah-see

books
livres
leevr
libros
lee-brohs
книги
k'nee-ghee

dresser
commode
koh-mohd
tocador
toh-kah-dohr
комод
kah-mohd

bed
lit
lee
cama
kah-mah
кровать
krah-vaht'

or Marseilles

sink

évier
eh-v'yeh

fregadero
freh-gah-deh-roh

кухонная раковина
koo-khon-nah-yah rah-kah-vee-nah

cupboard

buffet
bew-feh

aparador
ah-pah-rah-dohr

шкаф для посуды
shkahf dl'yah pah-soo-dee

glasses

verres
vehr

vasos
vah-sohs

стаканы
stah-kah-nee

plates

assiettes
ah-s'yeht

platos
plah-tohs

тарелки
tah-r'yehl-kee

Barcelona

window
fenêtre
fuh-nehtr
ventana
vehn-tah-nah
окно
ahk-noh

table
table
tahbl
mesa
meh-sah
стол
stohl

spoons
cuillères
kwee-yehr
cucharas
koo-chah-rahs
ложки
loh-shkee

stove
cuisinière
kwee-zee-n'yehr
cocina
koh-thee-nah
плита
plee-tah

bowl
bol
bohl
tazón
tah-thohn
миска
mees-kah

or Leningrad

sofa

divan
dee-vahn

sofá
soh-fah

диван
dee-vahn

curtains

rideaux
ree-doh

cortinas
kohr-tee-nahs

занавески
zah-nah-v'yeh-skee

pillows

oreillers
oh-reh-yeh

almohadones
ahl-moh-ah-doh-nehs

подушки
pah-doosh-kee

chair

chaise
shehz

silla
seel-yah

стул
stool

To be at home is always fun, but it is especially exciting when family and friends come to visit.

There is so much to do before the party begins . . .

in Chicago

cook

cuisiner
kwee-zee-neh

cocinar
koh-thee-nahr

варить
vah-reet'

bake

cuire
kweer

hornear
ohr-neh-ahr

печь
p'yehch

decorate

décorer
deh-koh-reh

decorar
deh-koh-rahr

украшать
oo-krah-shaht'

or Marseilles

sweep

balayer
bah-leh-yeh

barrer
bah-rrehr

подметать
pahd-m'yeh-taht

set the table

mettre la table
mehtr lah tahbl

poner la mesa
poh-nehr lah meh-sah

накрывать на стол
nah-kree-vaht' nah stohl

Barcelona

brush the teeth

se brosser les dents
suh broh-seh leh dahng

cepillarse los dientes
theh-pee-l'yahr-seh lohs d'yehn-tehs

чистить зубы
chee-steet' zoo-bee

wash

se laver
suh lah-veh

lavarse
lah-vahr-seh

умываться
oo-mee-vah-tsah

or Leningrad

comb

peigner
peh-n'yeh

peinar
pay-nahr

причёсывать
pree-ch'yoh-see-vhat'

dress

s'habiller
sah-b'yeh

vestirse
vehs-teer-seh

одеваться
ah-d'yeh-vah-tsah

The guests arrive!

Mother serves many
delicious foods
at the party...

in Chicago

butter
beurre
buhr
mantequilla
mahn-teh-kee-l'yah
масло
mah-slah

soup
soupe
soop
sopa
soh-pah
суп
soop

milk
lait
leh
leche
leh-cheh
молоко
mah-lah-koh

salt
sel
sehl
sal
sahl
соль
sohl

pepper
poivre
pwahvr
pimienta
pee-m'yehn-tah
перец
p'yeh-r'yehts

or Marseilles

peas

petits pois
p'tee pwah

guisantes
ghee-sahn-tehs

зелёный горошек
z'yeh-l'yoh-nee gah-roh-sheck

potatoes

pommes de terre
pohm duh tehr

patatas
pah-tah-tahs

картофель
car-toh-f'yehl'

fish

poisson
pwah-sohng

pescado
pehs-kah-doh

рыба
ree-bah

bread

pain
pehng

pan
pahn

хлеб
khl'yehp

Barcelona

water
eau
oh
agua
ah-gwah
вода
vah-dah

olives
olives
oh-leev
olivas
oh-lee-vahs
маслины
mah-slee-nee

chicken and rice
poulet au riz
poo-leh oh ree
arroz con pollo
ah-rroth kohn poh-l'yoh
цыплёнок с рисом
tsee-plyoh-nahk s'ree-sahm

or Leningrad

fruit
fruit
frwee
fruta
froo-tah
фрукты
frook-tee
tea
thé
teh
té
teh
чай
chigh
sugar
sucre
sewkr
azúcar
ah-thoo-kahr
сахар
sah-khahr
pastry
pâtisserie
pah-tee-sree
pasteles
pahs-teh-lehs
печенье
p'yeh-ch'yeh-n'ye

Everyone sings and laughs and tells funny stories as they sit around the table and enjoy one another's company...

in Chicago

father
papa
pah-pah
papá
pah-pah
папа
pah-pah

sister
soeur
suhr
hermana
ehr-mah-nah
сестра
s'yeh-strah

aunt
tante
tahnt
tía
tee-ah
тётя
t'yoh-t'yah

or Marseilles

uncle
oncle
ohnkl
tío
tee-oh
дядя
d'yah-d'yah

mother
maman
mah-mahng
mamá
mah-mah
мама
mah-mah

grandfather
grand-père
grahn-pehr
abuelo
ah-bweh-loh
дедушка
d'yeh-doosh-kah

grandmother
grand'mère
grahn-mehr
abuela
ah-bweh-lah
бабушка
bah-boo-shkah

Barcelona

great-grandmother

arrière grand'mère
ah-r'yehr grahn-mehr

bisabuela
bee-sah-bweh-lah

прабабушка
prah-bah-boosh-kah

cousins

cousins
koo-zehng

primos
pree-mohs

двоюродные
dvah-you-rahd-nee-yeh

brother

frère
frehr

hermano
ehr-mah-noh

брат
braht

or Leningrad

friend

amie
ah-mee

amiga
ah-mee-gah

приятельница
pree-yah-t'yehl-nee-tsah

neighbors

voisins
vwah-zehng

vecinos
veh-thee-nohs

соседи
sah-s'yeh-dee

On quiet days
when it rains or snows
and you cannot go
outside there is
always something
to do . . .

in Chicago

paint

peindre
pehndr

pintar
peehn-tahr

рисовать красками
ree-sah-vaht krah-skah-mee

build

construire
kohns-trweer

construir
kohns-troo-eer

строить
stroh-eat'

paste

coller
koh-leh

pegar
peh-gahr

клеить
klyeh-eat'

or Marseilles

listen

écouter
eh-koo-teh

escuchar
ehs-koo-chahr

слушать
sloo-shaht

play

jouer
zhoo-eh

jugar
hoo-gahr

играть
ee-graht'

Barcelona

read

lire
leer

leer
leh-ehr

читать
chee-taht'

embroider

broder
broh-deh

bordar
bohr-dahr

вышивать
vee-shee-vaht'

or Leningrad

explore

explorer
ehks-ploh-reh

explorar
ehks-ploh-rahr

исследовать
ees-sl'yeh-dah-vaht'

But no matter where you go, to distant places or just around the corner, it always feels good to come back home to Chicago or Marseilles, Barcelona or Leningrad.

Additional Words

home	maison *meh-zohng*	casa *kah-sah*	дома *doh-mah*
family	famille *fah-mee*	familia *fah-mee-l'yah*	семья *s'yeh-m'yah*
rooms	pièces *p'yehs*	cuartos *kwahr-tohs*	комнаты *koh-mnah-tee*
bedroom	chambre à coucher *shahmbr ah koo-sheh*	dormitorio *dohr-mee-toh-r'yoh*	спальня *spah-l'n'yah*
kitchen	cuisine *kwee-zeen*	cocina *koh-thee-nah*	кухня *koo'kh-n'yah*
living room	salle de séjour *sahl duh seh-zhoor*	sala *sah-lah*	гостиная *gah-stee-nah'yah*
party	réception *reh-sehp-s'yohng*	fiesta *f'yehs-tah*	вечеринка *v'yeh-ch'yeh-reen-kah*
visit	visite *vee-zeet*	visita *vee-see-tah*	посещение *pah-s'yeh-shch'yeh-nee-yeh*
guests	invités *ehng-vee-teh*	invitados *een-vee-tah-dohs*	гости *goh-stee*
Chicago	Chicago *shee-kah-go*	Chicago *chee-kah-goh*	Чикаго *chee-kah-gah*
Marseilles	Marseille *mahr-seh*	Marsella *mahr-seh-l'yah*	Марсель *mahr-s'yehl'*
Barcelona	Barcelone *bahr-suh-lon*	Barcelona *bahr-theh-loh-nah*	Барселона *bahr-s'yeh-loh-nah*
Leningrad	Leningrad *leh-neen-grahd*	Leningrado *leh-neehn-grah-doh*	Ленинград *l'yeh-neen-grahd*

Russian Alphabet

А	а	ah as in arch
Б	б	b as in boy
В	в	v as in voice
Г	г	g as in good
Д	д	d as in do
Е	е	yeh as in yet
Ё	ё	yoh as in yoyo
Ж	ж	zh as in pleasure
З	з	z as in zero
И	и	ee as in feet
Й	й	y as in yeast
К	к	k as in keep
Л	л	l as in luck
М	м	m as in me
Н	н	n as in now
О	о	oh as in often when stressed, closer to ah when unstressed
П	п	p as in pie
Р	р	r as in porridge
С	с	s as in stay
Т	т	t as in toy
У	у	oo as in foot
Ф	ф	f as in fix
Х	х	kh as in hot
Ц	ц	ts as in let's go
Ч	ч	ch as in church
Ш	ш	sh as in short
Щ	щ	shch as in borshch
Ъ	ъ	separation sign (')
Ы	ы	ih as in a drawn-out is
Ь	ь	soft sign (preceding consonant pronounced as if ee followed)
Э	э	eh as in empty
Ю	ю	yuh as you
Я	я	yah as in yard

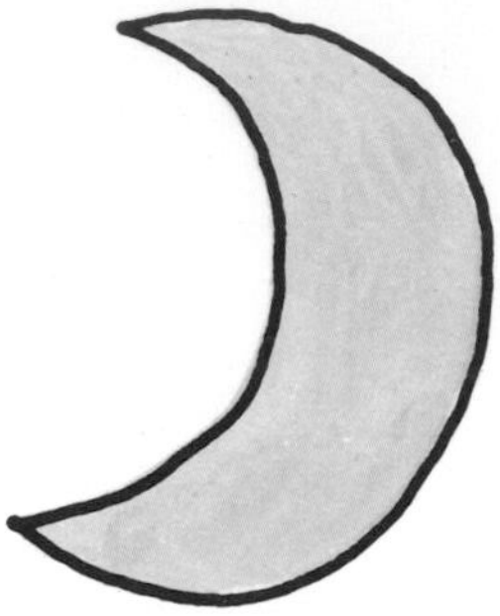

the end

fin

fin

коне́ц